YOUR KNOWLEDGE H⸢

- We will publish your bachelor's and
  master's thesis, essays and papers

- Your own eBook and book -
  sold worldwide in all relevant shops

- Earn money with each sale

Upload your text at www.GRIN.com
and publish for free

Forerunning Value Mechanics In Value Science And Theory. The Discovery, Verification, & Justification Of The Model Of Universality Of Value & Its Sensitivity

Wisdom Yao Dornyo

Bibliographic information published by the German National Library:

The German National Library lists this publication in the National Bibliography; detailed bibliographic data are available on the Internet at http://dnb.dnb.de.

ISBN: 9783346289636
This book is also available as an ebook.

© GRIN Publishing GmbH
Nymphenburger Straße 86
80636 München

Print and binding: Books on Demand GmbH, Norderstedt, Germany
Printed on acid-free paper from responsible sources.

The present work has been carefully prepared. Nevertheless, authors and publishers do not incur liability for the correctness of information, notes, links and advice as well as any printing errors.

GRIN web shop: https://www.grin.com/document/948079

FORERUNNING
VALUE MECHANICS
IN VALUE SCIENCE AND THEORY 1
$$[V + B \leq U + S]$$

**THE DISCOVERY, VERIFICATION, AND JUSTIFICATION OF
THE MODEL OF UNIVERSALITY OF VALUE AND ITS SENSITIVITY**

WISDOM YAO DORNYO (PHD, MBA)

FORERUNNING VALUE MECHANICS

SYSTEMS SCIENCE AND THEORY VOLUME I

[THE VALUE THEORY]

FOCUSING

THE DISCOVERY, VERIFICATION, & JUSTIFICATION OF THE MODEL OF UNIVERSALITY

OF VALUE & ITS SENSITIVITY

$(v + b \leq u + s)$

BY

WISDOM YAO DORNYO

OCTOBER, 2020

Contents

ABSTRACT

The introduction to value sensitivity was much digested to serve its intended reason as the core fundamental to support the superstructure of the thesis. The model of flexibility also known as the model of universality was hypothesized and tested through various experiments with figures and found to rationally agreeing with value cores and characteristics of a system. The essence of language as a structure very important to everything as well as waves are concerned was outlined. Waves is everything we could see and hear and touch, thus, also, wave is sound, light, heat, the unseen, and this is digital. The model of universality was used to better understand Amdahl, Gustafson-Barsis, etc. with their theoretical system speedup latency theories. The model of universality was further pursued to arrive at an expression for value as $v = -n^2$, where n is the number of trials to enhance a system and v is value. In fact, there is seemingly numerous approaches to establishing a mechanics of value which is a whole subject that could be studied as a program. Further research on value and its sensitivity lies ahead. Studying anything rather indirectly by means of its value trends makes a deeper understanding.

DEDICATION

To my daughter Lydia Emefa Abra Dornyo, my son Prince Mawutor Kofi Intellect Dornyo, my wife Iveta Dornyo Zajicova, my mother Comfort Afua Dza, and my father Alex Kwasi Dornyo

ACKNOWLEDGEMENT

To all my lecturers, supervisors, and advisors. We are also highly grateful to all owners of intellectual properties which we have used to help shape this work into the current pattern and excellence. Thank you all!

CHAPTER 1

INTRODUCTION

1.0 INTRODCTION: Attempts have been made to develop a hypothetical basic model to help view the subject fundamentally, so as to make flexible blends with other schools of thought and to serve as a tool of analysis of measure of enhanced value and hence performance measure. It was realized that a holistic view of the subject demanded diversified subjects of taught for completeness. The developed model would serve as an interface, a buffer and a master key among other models existing. The performance measured was considered in this work as existing in discrete levels of measured value equaled the enhanced value, an overall efficiency, taken individual efficiencies of a valuable entity or system. Hopefully, this model would play an essential role in originally contributing to knowledge and empirical deductions in value enhancement evaluation.

1.1 INTRODUCTION TO VALUE SENSITIVITY WITH RESPECT TO THE BUFFER MODEL OF PERFORMANCE MEASUREMENT (BMPM) [THE BMPM IS ALSO KNOWN AS THE MODEL OF UNIVERSALITY ACCORDING TO THIS PROJECT WORK]

To a person a basic is the universal set of a valuable or valuables that he/she considers as demanding a form of enhancement in value status. It could be raw materials for building construction or it could be a completed building but pending yet another round or further other rounds of renovation (re-innovation) so as to put it at the next level of enhanced status. This enhanced status equals enhanced valuable, and an enhanced valuable has an enhanced value, and an enhanced value means added value. Because the demand for that form of enhancement in value status is fulfilled, it is likely that human demand for the valuable (commodity) will increase. In this case the law of demand and supply in economics comes into play.

Definition: We view the topic above as the design of a sensitive means of analysis of enhanced value considering human performance embedded in or embodying valuables, systems and achievements using scientific methodologies to qualify and quantify empirical theoretical models and technological frameworks to that effect.

In other words as stated above, value is in valuable and valuable is obtained by achievement or nature. Achievement is in performance and the level of achievement depends on the level and quality of performance.

Can we measure performance and therefore achievement? If so then we can know the level of a valuable and we can separate the value from the valuable to know the difference (a residue) or a basic or vice versa in order to know the level of the value. The level of the value is the magnitude of the valuable. The critical process to obtain these levels is the sensitive evaluation of value a design to be designed. The above shows that value and a difference (a residue) give a valuable plus something (x) but x should be something and the thing must be flexible to have a changing effect on the valuable. According to the view of this paper, the most suitable term to give this flexible something is 'slack'. This can be seen as a model a flexible model and therefore a buffer. This is then a buffer model.

Value (v) plus basic (b) is less than or equals valuable (u) plus slack (s) ---- (1). Rewriting it, we have the following: $v + b \leq u + s$ ---- (1).

In this paper the model defined is viewed as a 'considered level of which the level is the measured magnitude which is reached as a result of adding values to the basics of an entity, system etc. by the power of a slack to reach higher other levels, where the slack is considered to be a force of change. The change is that element of flexibility that promotes entrepreneurial elements such as innovations, new technologies, inventions/ discoveries and creativities of change. The level as mentioned earlier which is the measured magnitude and which is the performance level is the measure of the value in a valuable considering performance.

The model has the RHS - right hand side (valuable plus slack) and the LHS – left hand side (value plus basics). The RHS of the model implies the added value to the basic plus the slack. This added value is subject to further enhancement to other higher discrete levels because of the element of slack there that affects it. This shows that, a lower discrete level is subject to rising to a higher discrete level and higher and higher in the upwards direction or vice versa depending on the slack.

8

The LHS of the model represents a basic entity, system, life, a good, service or commodity or an object to which level is enhanced or is to be enhanced by adding value. The process, 'adding value', goes into forming a valuable (a valuable entity, system, life, good or service).

From the model above, if there is slack = 0, then value (v) + basic (b) ≤ valuable (u) + 0, therefore, v + b = u ---- (2), but if there is available slack = 1, 2, 3, and so on, then, the valuable (u) is affected by this slack = 1. Slack = 1 implies s_1, we then have a new model, an inequality, that is, $v + b \leq u + s_1$ ---- (3). If there is slack = 2 then, $u + s_1 \leq u_1 + s_2$ ---- (4), and for slack = 3 we have $u_1 + s_2 \leq u_2 + s_3$ ---- (5), where $s \rightarrow v$ thus, the s tends to behaving like v giving similar infinite chain reaction in ascending order. Since slack has a changing effect on a basic and value also has a changing effect on a basic, both of them can interchange or replace each other that is why we see the right hand side of the preceding inequalities being repeated in the left hand side of the proceeding inequalities as seen above. In further clarifying, $v + b = u$ is such that $v + b \leq u + s_1$, so that $u + s_1 \leq u_1 + s_2$, ... where v which is the value implies now as, s_1, s_2, s_3 ... but not equal to any of these slacks, that is, v is actually less than any of them in magnitude, and also, similarly as of v, b which is the basic implies u_1, u_2, u_3 ... but not equal to any of these valuables in magnitude. In fact, the enhanced b is the new u i.e. the new valuable. In this case, the slack behaves as though it is a value which effects a change on the basic, and the valuable behaves as though it is the basic which is being changed into a higher status. Slack = 0 implies there is no innovation to improve the current basic or valuable at hand, however, slack = 1, 2, 3, and so on shows that there is or are innovations to advance technology for the improvement of the current basic or valuable at hand. The later also shows the level reached of performance, achievement, value and valuable of an entity, system, or a personality.

The right hand side (RHS) of the inequalities above where we have slack = s_1, s_2, s_3 and so on, indicate that there is the potential that valuables u, u_1, u_2 and so on, have statuses which could be enhanced technologically through knowledge, creativity and innovations. However, if at any stage of the respective inequalities slack = 0, then we have equations instead of inequalities such as in equation (2) above, and further, $v + b < u + s_1$ as in equation (3) above, but where $s_1 = 0$, then $v + b = u$: also, $u + s_1 < u_1 + s_2$ as in equation (4) above, but where $s_2 = 0$, then $u + s_1 = u_1$: and when $u_1 + s_2 < u_2 + s_3$ as in

9

equation (5) above, however, where $s_3 = 0$, then $u_1 + s_2 = u_2$. Where the symbol < means "less than", and ≤ means "less than or equal to".

Why chosen the very topic? A general view of the main theme, Value Design Evaluation and its Sensitivity, indicated that, it cuts across board scientific (social sciences e.g. economics, physical or natural science, where emphasis on derivation of empirical deductions and their synthesis and analysis are touched through hypothesis, experimentations, conclusions and models for onward theories to be arrived at expectedly), technology as of those in information systems and their management strategies as in human organizational management systems and internet systems, computer systems, databases and interphase language systems such as c++, java, etc. also, knowledge systems, creativity and innovations. It was realized that stages of original contribution to knowledge would be arrived at with the theme specified as shown in the specifically focused main topic above. As seen in the specifically focused topic, the mechanics of value sensitivity of designs of evaluation methodology would follow four strategies such as;

1. The scientific method
2. Human level attained
3. Human attitude towards a valuable entity
4. Use of statistically quantitative and qualitative management decision making tools to analyze and synthesize 1, 2, 3 above.

The hope was to have a model, see the model above. This was meant to serve as one of the evaluation tools to facilitate and behave as an interphase, a buffer, and a master key, taking into consideration the evaluation methodologies above and the various human and information systems. In evaluating value and for that matter performance, the accuracy (quality) of work or task finished, time used to finish the task, cost of the task or valuable obtained from executing the task, and demand for the valuable would be taken into consideration. Whatever value in performance that should be evaluated should be given a test to see whether it is observed positively or negatively. How? One of these methods is by selling (displaying) it; the idea is to see the observed attitude of a defined society towards it. This would make

10

us sometimes adjust (slack) in a direction in favor of the society so as to pull demand and hence supply. Value and performance is firstly considered and defined by an individual, and secondly by the defined society observing the task, and thirdly by taking cue from the first and the second above, and then a system or a social or a scientific mechanism or model is designed to help easily execute similar cases.

1.2 THE SCIENTIFIC METHOD

This will include all the scientific methodologies necessary and will be used in the paper. That is; hypothesis, observation, measurement, experimentation, formulation, controlled experimentation testing and modification of hypothesis. According to Sciencebuddies.org, David Schwartz (1923-2012) "The scientific method is a way to ask and answer questions by making observations and doing experimentations. The steps are; ask a question, do background research, construct a hypothesis, test your hypothesis by doing an experiment, Analyze your data and draw a conclusion, communicate your results."

1.3 HUMAN LEVEL ATTAINED

This is classified under knowledge (academic credentials, academic contributions and knowledgeable creativities), wealth (monetary wealth, collateral, and infrastructure), and authority (style and power; i.e. style- social life style and cultural life style, power-financial power, economic power and political power).

1.3.0 Knowledge: This includes academic credentials, academic contributions and knowledgeable creativities.

1.3.1 Academic Credentials: This will include the human level of education as a pure academician or as a professionally skilled trained, also, achievements in terms of course grades and the class of certificates truly obtained. Amount of workshops and seminars attended and professional experience in relation to one's areas of studies which is acquired after school.

Also, the sum total of all areas of programs of studies and the enhanced change in the person to face tasks and the extent of capability to solve problems of those fields of studies or other fields.

1.3,2 Academic Contributions: This includes contributions such as deductions of models, principles, theories and laws for publication to scientific journals and authorship of books for publication to be used by students and instructors. 'Academic contributions' also involves ideas, proposals or other articles written to show the way or direct a course to the solution of an educational problem or initiation of an educational project which is published or submitted. Teaching in an effective manner also shows the level of contribution made to knowledge.

1.3.3 Knowledgeable Creativities: This includes discoveries, inventions, and innovations where there is an indication of original contributions to knowledge and amount of books or articles written and published for the purpose of human education or for technology and scientific advancement. Creativities such as the internet and the pc that empowered human in order to enhanced knowledge.

1.3.4 Wealth: This involves monetary wealth, collateral, and infrastructure. **Monetary Wealth:** This is made up of liquidity, money in cash at hand. **Collateral:** This will include achievements in terms of acquisition of collaterals and financial investments and shareholding. Also, the amount of acquisition of land buildings, plants and machineries show the amount of wealth. **Infrastructure:** valuable contributions to an economy such as built schools and social amenities, efficient roads and bridges, diversified transportation systems, auditoriums and buildings in general.

1.3.5 Authority: This includes style and power.

Style: Style includes social life style and the cultural life style of the people living in a particular geographical area including their spoken languages. These are very important styles for anybody to adapt to, in order to sound and seem sensitive to the system. It makes one active to propel progress and survive the system in question. It paves the way and brings ease, flexibility and success to adaptors of the styles. It is easy or the probability could be higher to control and govern the system having studied and adjusted and innovatively used the social and cultural life styles of the system and the people. The style of a people gripped and taken advantage of helps one to attain the enhanced value to the satisfaction of the people in that area. It increases respect, trust and high expectations of the people in that area for that person. **Social life style:** This appertains to the social life styles of the people in a system. **Cultural life style:** This appertains to the cultural life styles of the people in a system.

Power: This includes financial power, economic power and political power. **Financial power** includes the capacity of finances of an entity. **Economic power** includes **microeconomic power** and **macroeconomic power**. With **political power**, a ruler has power and an enhanced value of authority. The repose of voting trust in a person to occupy a position depends on how best he or she played politics to that effect.

1.4 HUMAN ATTITUDE TOWARDS A VALUABLE ENTITY
This shows the amount of demand for that entity. The higher the demand the more the enhanced value and vice versa

1.5 USE OF QUANTITATIVE AND QUALITATIVE MANAGEMENT DECISION MAKING TOOLS TO ANALYZE AND SYNTHESIZE THE PREVIOUS METHODOLOGIES
This includes the use of applied statistics to design and evaluate the three methodologies stated above.

1.6 THE BUFFER MODEL OF PERFORMANCE MEASUREMENT (BMPM)
Why 'buffer'? A buffer according to the Oxford Advanced Learner's dictionary is defined as „a thing or a person that reduces a shock or protects somebody or something against difficulties". This explains the model as a fundamental one which is to make flexible blends with other advanced treatments and serves as a tool of analysis. It focuses an understanding or agreement among them e.g. considering the model as a hypothetical platform, a statement of Peter Drucker in the research paper of (Mihir A, 2006) that referred to Drucker's Harvard Business Review article, could be explained or analyzed. This states that, "until a business returns a profit that is greater than its cost of capital, it operates at a loss. Never mind that it pays taxes as if it had a genuine profit. The enterprise still returns less to the economy than it devours... until then it does not create wealth, it destroys it". Over here the (model's) four terms value, basic, valuable, and slack, have been used to analyze Drucker's statement. The business's profit is the value in the valuable which could be achieved through the process of returning a profit. That is, **adding**

13

value to the cost of capital (the basic). Without that much profit, Drucker wrote that the business operates at a loss. All the remaining extras in the statement could be the slack which is obligation due to tax payment. As a result the business's extent of wealth created depends on innovative approaches (slack) used. Without a genuine cutting-edge mechanism, crude managerial strategy (ineffective slack manipulations) would instead destroy the wealth.

Drucker's statement above was also, confirmed by Pamela Peterson Drake (1997) that, "we say that a firm has added value over a period of time when it has; generated a profit in excess of a firm's cost of capital." Therefore, that profit which could be affected by the slack is value added or added value. If the slack is zero the added value is at a discrete level equals a performance measure but if the slack is more than zero, a higher discrete level is reached giving a higher magnitude of the performance measure. According to Daimler, "value added is one element of the performance measurement system (Pmt) and is calculated as the difference between operational results and the cost of capital of the average net assets in that period"The profit (INVESTOPEDIA, 2013) referred above is the "economic profit".

This example is only about economic profit. There are diversified instances that could be highlighted by using the model. In this paper, added value as noted earlier is related to performance and therefore performance measure which relates to value evaluation and not only in economics or accounting but also relating to other social sciences, science and technology where knowledge, creativity, and innovations are brought to play. For this paper, whether we are using added value or value added, we are just trying to drive at a common goal that is value sensitive design of evaluation in various systems as noted in the thesis topic above.

1.7 PERFORMANCE MEASUREMENT (VALUE EVALUATION)

This according to this work is the process of determining the value or magnitude of an act, action, characteristics, level or might, or performance of something. E.g. Sales targets hit within a stipulated period of time, examination scores, durability and maneuverability of a machine, speed of moving bodies or machines, information technology systems and management systems, achievements of humans, human rights and integrity and welfare and justice systems or entities. According to William

M. K. Trochim, (2006), "measurement is the process of observing and recording the observations that are collected as part of a research effort". At Mathsfun website (2011), measurement is defined as "finding a number that shows the size of amount of something". The Online Cambridge Dictionary (2011), defined measurement as "the act or process of measuring". Again, the Oxford Dictionary Online (2011) defined measurement as "the action of measuring something". For all the above definitions we can see common words such as action, process, extent, finding, value, and something. Applying these words, performance measurement can be defined as 'the act or process of finding the extent of value of performance where performance implies the action of something'. Hence performance measurement is a process and performance measure is the value of something which again as stated already in the introduction above, lies in a level which implies the value added and which can shift from one discrete level to another discrete level through adjustments effected by a change due to flexibility. This can be new knowledge discovered or innovations on or further funding of something.

1.8 AREAS WHERE PERFORMANCE MEASURE IS REQUIRED

Performance measure is applicable in education, sports, politics, economy, culture, society, technology and science, health, transportation, tourism and hospitality, and business. [UKESSAYS.COM (2003), James Raath (2007), Scott (2013)], wrote articles on key performance areas (KPA's) common to all businesses that determines the competitive differentiation. They stated that six areas can be measured and analyzed. These are;

"**Aspirational Index:** It is a measure of a company or team's belief in its people as the differentiating force of its business, and serves as aspirational benchmark of people's potential engagement in the financial improvement of the business when all other KPA's are applied. **Leadership Index:** It is the measure of the nature of influence of the organization in business by its leaders. A company's fortune lies entirely in the hands of its leaders at every level and their capacity to influence organizational engagement in the business. **'H' Factor Index:** Measures the deep-seated values and emotional intelligence of people and how well they express themselves creatively and purposefully in solving problems and building relationships as a means to delivering customer impact. [UKESSAYS.COM (2003), James Raath (2007), Scott (2013)], further wrote that, it as well as measures the 'mindset' and

15

'behavioral' deficits that impede elite performance in a team or organization. **Risk/ Reward Index:** This is the measure of the extent people in an organization share organizational risks and rewards. **The innovative Index:** This measures how innovative a company is. **The Customer Impact Index:** This shows the passion that customers have and how ready they are to protect the interest and brand of the organization they deal with. [UKESSAYS.COM (2003), James Raath (2007), Scott (2013)], posited that "Lack of customers impact impedes organizational progress" Some examples of KPAs are; training, management, purchases, Research and development, administration, finance, human resources, manufacturing, quality control, marketing and sales. The KPAs explained above is not complete without looking at key performance indicators (KPIs).

1.9 KPIs – KEY PERFORMANCE INDICATORS (KSIs - KEY SUCCESS INDICATORS)

Reh (2013) stated that, KPIs "help an organization to define and measure progress toward organizational goals. Once an organization has analyzed its mission, identified all its stake holders, and defined its goals, it needs a way to measure progress toward those goals" Reh (2013), posited that "KPIs are different with different organizations e.g. for a business it could be the percentage of its income, with a school it could be the graduation rate of its students, for a customer service department it could be the number of calls answered in the first minute and for a social service department it could be the number of clients assisted. He opined that KPIs are **long term** considerations and that they must reflect **organizational goals** and must be **key to its success**, and is **quantifiable** (measurable)"

etc KPIs are also "a combination that includes reports, spreadsheets, or charts. Sales figures and trends, over-time, personnel statistics and trends, supply chain information". Whatever is capable of a means to summarize raw data are indicators? Examples are; quantitative which deals with figures, directional which deals with the extent of betterment or not of an organization, practical which deals with interface between existing organizational processes, actionable which deals with an organization's capability to effect changes, and financial indicators which are used in indicating PM and operating index.

Some Examples of KPI: in the area of marketing are, new customer acquisition, demographic information, status of existing customers, turnover (revenue), outstanding balances held by segments of customers and payment terms, collection of bad debt, profitability of customers looking at their

16

demographic background and vice versa. Another example is the use of the balance scorecard. The balance score card would not be treated but in future research work.

The probable question to rise up here is how does the buffer model agree with the ideas of other schools? Below shows how some areas discussed above is compatible with the BMPM.

1.10 COMPATIBILITY OF THE BUFFER MODEL AND OTHER SCHOOLS OF THOUGHT

The answer to the question above is how compatible the terms of other schools of thought could be with the terms of the model. Also, the model is an equation and if so, does it agree with other equations either as a whole with regards to the whole equation or partly at just the LHS or the RHS. For example, as an equation, Daimler.com stated that **"value added = profit measure – net asset x cost of capital %"** also, **"value added = return on sale x net asset productivity – cost of capital x net asset"**.

Linking this to the buffer model,

Value added = valuable + slack – basics, and hence **valuable + slack – basics = profit measure – net asset x cost of capital % = return of sales – net asset productivity – cost of capital % x net asset**.

A lot of switches could be done with the model as a whole equation and as in blend with other equations as could be seen above. This could lead to a lot of deductions.

1.10.0 Future Research: One of the goals is to pursue experiments with the model as an equation to arrive at new deductions. Also to know whether value added should be a multiple or an addition (an additive). Since the model is a hypothetical type, it would be too early to draw conclusions unless experiments are done to arrive at empirical replicates or formulas that will prove certainties with figures. However, the model at the moment is playing a vital role in that it could digest complex advanced statements and give it a fundamental reform as noted earlier with P. Drucker's statement about company profit making. Also, it has the capacity of absorbing technical terms since the inherent terms in it (value, basic, valuable and slack) are general terms and this is what gives it the capacity to; serve as a point or

17

source of reference to reach other models existing or yet to be, focus easy understanding, reduce complexity, help classify terms in other models, aid scientific integration and approach, serve as a tool of its own capacity that could analyze- synthesize- and calculate the value of performance and as noted earlier, serve as a language of understanding to other bodies of knowledge. Some bodies of knowledge among the lot are those emerging from Gene Amdahl, John Little, John L. Gustafson, Edwin H. Barsis, the Cartesian equation, etc.

1.11 SOME OF THE TERMS THAT ARE IN LINE WITH THE 'BUFFER MODEL OF PERFORMANCE MEASUREMENT (BMPM)'

These are; profit, credibility, light, shape, operation, color, excellence, elegance, authenticity, material, substance, human, commodity, service(s), sound, waves, goods, skills, programs, styles, vision, objectives, operation, system, productivity, elegance etc. These terms would further be classified under the various terms in the BMPM developed.

1.12 THE BMPM DEVELOPED

This is where the various terms of the BMPM is treated separately. Future Research: Various means of using the BMPM will be tried out in a future research work in order to make it applicable as one of its goals. Let's look at the development of the four terms of the model.

1.12.0 VALUE

Value (Investorwords.com, 2013) is defined as "worth, desirability or utility". According to business dictionary.com (2013), value is "1. **Accounting:** The monetary worth of an asset, business entity, or liability or obligation acquired. 2. **Economics:** The worth of all the benefits and rights arising from ownership. Two types of economic value are (a) the utility of a good or service and (b) power of a good or service to command other goods, services, or money in voluntary exchange. 3. **Marketing:** The extent to which a good or service is perceived by its customer to meet his or her needs or want, measured by customer's willingness to pay for it. It commonly depends more on the customer's perception of the worth of the product than on its intrinsic value. 4. **Mathematics:** A magnitude or quantity represented by numbers" "Theory of value falls into two categories; (a) **intrinsic:** (objective) theory which holds

18

that the price of goods and services is not a function of subjective judgments but it is inherent in the objective nature of the good and how it came to being . (b) **Subjective theories:** These hold that for an object to have economic value (a non- zero price), the object must be useful in satisfying human wants and it must be in limited supply. This is the foundation of the marginal-list's theory of value. The marginal utility is not a normative theory of value. Hence what are being addressed are general prices. That is, the aggregate, not a specific price of a specific good or service in a given circumstance."

The definitions of value above showed value is an activator with power capable of enhancing basic standards. If the standards of basics are raised by value then some amount of work must be done to achieve that and we can see this in power. This is because there is working in power which should be accomplished over a unit time. This is what activates the level which is **profitable**. Value in this case is added to basics that is, **'value added'** and hence work done (performance) over a unit time is the measure of performance.

This **profit** is a desirable worth and utility as stated in the first definition of value above. This is a good or service whose value is enhanced to appeal to people so that they can patronize it. This can be seen in the second definition above. Subsequent definitions on value seen above show that value is money and it is also a human with an enhanced standard in various ways with respect to each valuable personality. It is a magnitude that should be quantified and it is a fundamental term having a universal power.

The following are some terms that could be placed under value; profit, credibility, light, shape, color, excellence, clearance, authenticity, etc.

1.12.1 BASICS
A basic can be matter (it is anything that has weight and can occupy space) or human or goods and services. The above is further (Ivestopedia.com, 2013) stressed by the following definitions; "**commodities** is defined as a **basic** good in commerce that is interchangeable with other commodities of the same type. Commodities are most often used as inputs in the production of other goods or services". The term matter is a general and scientific term that encompasses almost everything in the universe except free (empty) space (vacuum) and services. In this case, commodities and basics all form

subsets under matter or vice versa, they can therefore be applied interchangeably. Also, the term basic has a wide range of applications. Investorwords.com (2013), defined commodities as "a physical substance, such as food, grains, and metals which is interchangeable with other products of the same type and which investors buy or sell, usually through futures contracts". Again according to the meridian-webster.com (2013), "a commodity is an economic good: as 1) (a) a product of agriculture or mining, (b) an article of commerce especially when delivered for shipment (commodities futures), (c) mass-produce unspecialized product (commodity chemicals or commodity memory chips), 2) (a) something useful or valued, (b) convenience advantage, 3) Obsolete: quantity, lot, 4) a good or service whose wide availability typically leads to smaller profit margin and diminishes the importance of factors (as brand name) other than price, 5) one that is subject to ready exchange or exploitation (Dictionary.reference.com ,2013), within a market (stars as individuals and as commodities of the film industry)". All these definitions have a wide scope of considerations and shows that the word basic is universal since it forms a subset of it. The term basic can therefore be proved of universality and fundamentality by considering the following definitions: The Cambridge dictionary online (2013), defined basics as "the simplest and most important facts, ideas or thing connected with something". The Thesaurus dictionary online (2013), sited some synonyms for basic such as "fundamentals, essentials, rudiments, ABCs, elements, principles, first steps, principia, nuts and bolts, nitty-gritty, brass tacks, the three Rs". Dicitionary.reference.com (2013), stated that, 'Basic' is referred to as "basic rudiments, basic principle, bedrock, fundamental principle. Also, of relating to, or forming the base or essence, or having the character of , or of, being, or serving as a starting point or basic, producing, resulting from, or relating to a base". The Oxford Dictionary Online (2013), defined basics as "forming an essential foundation or starting point; fundamental". Whereas, the term basics is part of the buffer model which focuses the strength of universality which puts it at the barest minimum to absorb whatever term connects with other schools about value added as performance measurement.

The following terms can be grouped under basics; substance, human, commodity, service, sound, waves, goods, skills, programs, styles, objectives, vision, mission, management, marketing, sales, productions, operations, systems, entities, etc. Let's look at the next term "valuable' in the BMPM.

20

1.12.2 VALUABLE

This is almost like of the term value but with a difference that, this value has blended with the basics of commodities being good or services or life or humans.

If we use a word such as profit for value, it will become a profitable for the term valuable "(a)ble" is added. E.g. 'Credibility' in value becomes 'a credible' in valuable. A term like 'shape' in value becomes 'a shaped' in valuable or color in value becomes 'a colored' in valuable, that is, 'ed' is added. The Oxford dictionary online (2013), defined valuable as "worth or great deal of money: a valuable antique, extremely useful or important, my time is valuable or a thing that is of great worth especially a small item of personal property". The Cambridge Dictionary online (2013), defined 'valuable' as, "worth a lot of money". Valuable is defined as "having considerable monetary worth or having qualities of esteem." Also, from Defitions.net (2013), we have "worthy esteem; as, a valuable friend; a valuable companion". The above definitions again showed that a valuable could be a commodity, a good, a service, or a person that has a great value embedded in a valuable therefore a valuable is a basic with an enhanced value known as value added which in turn implies a performance measure.

Should a question arise such as, what about for the worse? The answer is yes, it exists that the worse can be encountered on a valuable if the elements of slack were bad. This would make the valuable to become a liability instead of an asset, see the first definition of value under the term 'value' noted earlier in this paper which indicates a stress on this possibility. Again, it is evident that the term valuable is a fundamental word with universality there in inherent. Therefore, all the terms value basics and valuable are already flexible but could be further flexed by the power of a slack.

1.12.3 SLACK

This could be flexibility. That is, the element of flexibility that will accommodate holistic strategies, to enhance or add up further value and enhance valuables and to link up performance measurement framework strategies. It is the term that permits the compatibility of fast changes in information systems, technology, education, culture, socialization, economies and politics. Since n has a changing effect on u, then s could imply n, and v, respectively, since v changes b, and since b is a lower or another version of u.

21

Some terms that are in this case synonymous or implications to slack are; change, adjustment, innovation, improvement, risk, extent of advancement in technology, level of education and information, information technology and communication, top management and decision making, bench marks, availability of resources and finances. This is the mechanism that serves as a telescope to view the final product (people, goods, services etc.) and these final products are the valuable goods to whatever level. A measuring tool is then determined to be used to measure the finished products to see their extents of value.

The extents of value are then the performance level and the performance levels are the degrees that could be judged quantitatively and qualitatively using the appropriate body of knowledge, skills, and thought schools. In general, the use of a cutting edge technology to determine the value added and therefore the performance measure. All these boil down to aiding facilitation, recognition of performance level and the appropriate use of measuring tools in executing targeted goals.

These terms have been stated all over under value, basic, valuable and slack so that they find better placement.

1.13 THE TOOLS OF PERFORMANCE MEASUREMENT FRAME WORK AND THEIR USES

The tools or elements eva, mva, npv are economic and marketing tools, statistical tools such as quantitative and qualitative methods of business and other fields of importance, bench marks and standards, financial accounting and reporting strategies, innovative competitive strategies, operation and or product quality control and quantity, balance score card (this would be treated in detail in future research project concerning the topic during the PhD program).

In fact, these tools allow an entity to use any tool of measurements and comparisons to satisfy criteria level and value attached to structures, systems, goods and services. All the above methods are powerful but it is one aim of this paper to as well as **adds a new tool of measurement to the managerial tools**. Future Research: For space and time limitations, the use of some of these tools could be reserved for future research work which reflects the use of the BMPM itself as a tool of analyses and measurement of value and performance.

Future Research: This investigates deeply into other models and searches how it compares to other models. Future search into the BMPM further investigates its status (IBM) i.e. interface, buffer and master key.

1.13.0 As an interface (communication piece), it is the mediator, the common communicator between observer(s) other models that it links up and serves as a common language of understanding among all. 1.13.1 As a buffer (accommodator), it serves as a clean slate (tabula rasa) that has a high capacity of absorbing and agreeing with different shapes and patterns (principles and models) of other schools of thought.

1.13.2 As a master key, it has the ability to fitting into the different shapes and patterns that can be accommodated and agreed with by the BMPM. Note that the perfection of the model is not yet concluded but more room for improvement is left for future work. However, it is for the time being an apparatus that aids an initial standing point in classifying and analyzing issues on performance and therefore value enhancement.

Finally, the performance which is to be measured is therefore seen as **efficiency. Efficiency** which is an individual efficiency is therefore a measured output expressed over a measured input. In total, for an entity or a system, an overall performance must be measured in order to know its enhanced value or vice versa. An overall performance will therefore give rise to an overall efficiency which is the consideration of the sum total of a measured output and a measured input expressed as ratio or sum of (i.e. + or -), thus, the average of the individual efficiencies together. There could be defection to the positive (profit) or to the negative (loss) direction.

It pays when one at time, efficiency is considered first of all separately, and all together, then giving a complex (holistic) scope of the performance level measured of an entity or a system in terms of percentages. Hence a performance measure = enhanced value (added value) measured implies an efficiency expressed. An efficiency expressed is therefore the result of considering almost every element that can play an important part in the enhanced value evaluation process. The enhanced value evaluation process is the value enhancement process in order to elevate or achieve a particular standard.

1.14 A BRIEF LOOK INTO THE BUFFER MODEL ITSELF AS A TOOL OF ANALYSIS AND MEASUREMENT OF VALUE AND PERFORMANCE

Looking at the model, it shows that value (v) is a function of valuable (u), basic (b) and slack (s). This can be stated as value added $v = f(u, b, s)$ where b is negative in the function.

In real life situation, whatever gives us a profit is taken through some sort of project work. Some amount of work must be done therefore, and this is where the quantitative methods of business i.e. applied statistics is to be used in calculating the project crash time, labor (skilled or other), tasks or loads to clear, funding, start – finish times and project duration, profits to realize, etc.

For all these, the simple terms of the model are able to accommodate them. The profit here stands for the enhanced value, the funding capital stands for the basics, and the first overall outcome of the project stands for the valuable. Now,

Where lies the project itself and processes within, its design taken into consideration forecast, crash times, quantity and caliber of labor, quality control etc.? The answer is **slack**. It is the slack that stands for whatever innovations and technologies that must be brought into play during the project.

This is just one way of usage of the model but as flexible as the model is or would be, there are many ways where the tools of performance measure as stated above is foreseen to be used with. This is a task to find (research) into during the PhD program.

1.15 SUMMARY OF THE USEFULNESS OF THE BMPM AS A TOOL OF ANALYSIS OF VALUE AND PERFORMANCE

It helps to carryout analysis and classifications with regards to the main topic at hand, it has the needed linkages to aid holistic metrics in investigations of the main topic, it serves as a sort of interface capable of possible intercommunication among various schools of thought and models in existence, it is like a buffer, fluid enough, to allow inflation to extensive levels without unnecessarily bursting off (losing control), serves as common language used to facilitate comprehensive integration and solidarity among other models (an inter-models language).

Some already existing models are the first and the second generation of performance measurement frame works, which could not be treated in this work for now, but futures research will cater for those.

ABBREVIATIONS: PM (performance measure), PMt (performance measurement), P (performance), M (Measure), B-Model-PM (buffer model of performance measurement)

1.16 TASKS AHEAD

The following tasks are pending future work; 1) literature review, 2) expatiating on the methodology stated above, 3) draw questionnaire where applicable, 4) design experiment for the model, 5) give a diagrammatic representation of the model, 6) link the model to existing scientific principles and theories, 7) attempt to focus the experiment to information engineering, 8) arrive at empirical deductions, 9) attempt to design an information system and program it to evaluate value of a valuable entity or system, 10) develop parameters to test the values in certain selected areas in technology and management systems and design sensitive sub-models built on the buffer model to evaluate them (using statistics and mathematics), 11) link the evaluation to human performance, 12) suggest means to enhance human value through performance, 13) evaluate the enhanced value in existing completed advanced work of humans using natural science principles e.g. "slack" could as well as be viewed as a sort of potential −an energy that gives ability to execute tasks in order to enhance the value in the work done (where the ratio of energy input to execute the task, to that of energy output, equals efficiency of the task executing system). 14) Research and link some principles of management, economic, psychology, philosophy, and sociology to value evaluation in humans. 15) Finally, further experiment on the model and final conclusion ideas and theory.

All the above explanation simply shows that humans desire the best in everything we do, and we can achieve that through enhanced value. An enhanced value or an accomplished task means an achievement.

1.17 SYSTEMS SCIENCE AND FURTHER INTODUCTION TO VALUE SENSITIVITY

Systems have been defined according to the context of this paper as, "content procedure function contained". **Explanation:** A system must be open or closed. Also, a system must be functioning well or poor. An open system has one or more openings, the inlet and the outlet.

1.17.0 A SYSTEM WITH ONE OPENING: In some systems such as a bottle for instance, has just one opening and the same opening serves as the inlet and the outlet out of the bottle.

1.17.1 A SYSTEM WITH MORE THAN ONE OPENING: A more than one opening system for instance a burette has two openings i.e. the inlet into the burette and then the outlet of the burette which lets out the liquid inlet.

1.17.2 A CLOSE SYSTEM: A close system is forming a pin-pong ball. It is completely closed up with its internal system shielded from the outside environment to it by its shell (the boundary).

1.17.3 A SYSTEM BOUNDARY: Either an open or a closed system has a boundary. The boundary is the separation that makes it different from its surroundings.

1.17.4 THE DIFFERENTIATING SEPARATION: In case of an organization a community, or a locality, the separation is either the culture, codes, codes of conduct, set of rules and by laws, constitution, set plans, procedures, the whole content of the procedures of a system, functionality of the system, the containment. One or more of the above or all contained makes possible the separation of the system from its environment. This is what makes it different from its environment or from other systems. One or more or all of the above must be functioning to portray that system. A system therefore, as defined above must have all of; content, procedure, function, container, in order to be functioning. At least one must function to sustain or maintain-up the system.

1.17.5 SYSTEM PROCEDURES AND CONTENT: Simply, a system must have procedures, and must have, a content, and this content must be all those things (elements) in the system e.g. people, utilities, buildings, plants (physical and biological), movable things and trolleys, economy, politics, culture, rule of law and discipline, theories and practicalities (e.g. science and technology etc.) and the leader (management) of the system (SKOG). Where SKOG is S = system, K = knowledge, O = organization, G = government.

1.17.6 SYSTEM FUNCTIONALITY: In fact, the elements stated above function or must be functioning, for that system to be itself and be bounded, otherwise it is not bounded.

1.17.7 SYSTEM CONTAINER: The system must be contained in anything (accommodator) that tolerates it. In fact, the container of a system here could be seen as a tolerating one or the tolerance or the tolerance level. Every system has a tolerance level be it economic, political, cultural, social etc. otherwise it cannot exist as a system of or on its own. If a system does not exist on its own then, it is either non-existential or dependent.

1.17.8 A DEPENDENT SYSTEM: it is a system that depends on other system(s) or on other thing(s), e.g. an open system could be a dependent system. However, a close system exists on its own. A close system might be dependent depending on the nature of the system, maybe energy systems might depend on external energies e.g. the solar system. Our planet earth for instance is a system enclosed in the biosphere and the first surrounding space orbit. However, the earth receives energy from the sun. This is therefore, a close system that depends on an external energy the sun. An example of an independent close system is the pin-pong ball mentioned earlier. Systems are numerous in differences in nature even the atom, molecule, element, compounds, cells (physical, or biological), tissues, organs, fibers (plants), chromosomes and genes, stones, aquatic systems, and above all the ecosystems.

A stone for instance also fits the definition of content, procedures, function, contained, a physical system or a biological system as we read in the case of economics, political, cultural, and social systems (socio-economic and cultural or socio-cultural and political systems). For a system to function well and for a system to grow (a system grows into developed or advanced system) it must be engineered, and that calls for system engineering which means engineering a system. A system must be designed with all round capabilities and experiences such as, algorithmic (algorithmic system), economic, software engineering, mathematics and science, advanced technology, and engineering and technology in general and above all communication and information. Therefore, a systems engineer must be an all-round professional, or a gifted talent with results.

1.17.9 OTHER SYSTEMS: We have, thermodynamic systems, control engineering systems, systems engineering, biological systems, economic systems mechanical systems (engineering and computers) software, by various definitions, and a lot others not even stated here or remembered in this paper, In an earlier paper submitted for publication, "Micro-Macro Economics and management of IT", p…, and economics systems represented by the acronym, "STYLE". In another paper submitted for publication "Doctoral Seminar in Digital Economics and Management Research", we state the V+s where v = value, b = basics, V = valuable, and s = slack. In a third paper submitted for publication we expatiated "flexibility management", and all these work according to systems functions.

1.17.10 "STYLE" explains that an S = system, links up to its E = economy through the chain T = trend, Y = yield (anything good e.g. innovations, profits from trades, marketing, or anything progressive in an economy), light (information) and good education and effectiveness of news broadcasting, etc. and the economy itself are all the contents of the system and are contained in "STYLE" in the community. A system needs "SCIENCE" (S = seek, C = compare, I = inquiries, E = enhance, N = network, C = conclude, E = explain) to "REVAMP" it. Where REVAMP is (R = research, E = enhance, V = value, A = achievement, M = motivation, P = performance).

1.18 PEPERTUAL MODEL IN AN OPEN SYSTEM
1.18.0 AN OPEN SYSTEM: An open system has 1) input (basic), 2) output (valuable), and 3) adjustment (slack).

1.18.1 AN OPEN SYSTEM FOR INNOVATION: In this case, the first prototype or model depends on what? That is what has been innovated. 1) Is it a model? 2) Is it a hard/software mechanism? 3) Is it a statement or proposition? E.g. 1, 2, and 3, are all E = enhanced ideas. Their respective makeup is a respective content of pieces of information put together whether it is a hardware or software. Information is light = c. Light is expressed according to its brightness. The speed of light is $c = 3 \times 10^8 ms^{-1}$. Just as finance accounts for hardware or software in terms of money, an open system must account for hardware or software in terms of pieces of information as the first step in the system.

1.18.2 ANALYSIS: a) What? What system is it? That is, is it a model, hard/software mechanism or a statement (proposition)?

1.18.3 E.G: MODEL HARD/SOFTWARE MECHANISM, OR A STATEMENT/PROPOSITION
1.18.4 MODEL: A model can be a principle, idea, or a mental picture of a system mathematically or scientifically expressed. E.g. Einstein's theory of energy (E) is $E = mc^2$, Newton's third law is action and reaction are equal and opposite i.e. active force (F) = reactive force (R), F = R. In economics, Keynesian theory (we will slightly elaborate on this in another volume of this paper).

1.18.5 HARD/SOFTWARE MECHANISM: A physically visible model or prototype developed e.g. a mobile phone (smart phone), or a software developed e.g. Microsoft documents, database management systems, operating systems such as Android, Mac OS, Linux, Windows, BSD, IOS, IBM z/OS, Unix, etc. Operating systems. Source: Computer-Hope.com (copyright 2014).

1.18.6 PROPOSITION/STATEMENT: A statement or proposition that is scientific, economic, political, religious, or etc. to encourage social engineering and harmony. E.g. Moore's theory of CPU also of David House: "CPU power doubles every 18 months (David House)".

1.18.7 What is a system? 1) A group of interdependent items that interact regularly to perform a task. 2) An established or organized procedure: a method. 3) A computer system refers to the hardware and software components that run a computer or computers [Vangie Beal, (2014)].

1.19 INPUT, OUTPUT, ADJUSTMENT OPEN SYSTEMS

1.19.0 INTRODUCTION

Fig. 1 A hypothetically abstract model of a system based on the model of universality v + b = u + s, where s = 0, and in this case; v = value, b = basic, u = valuable, and s = slack.

Fig. 2. Further depiction of the hypothetically abstract model of a system with replacement of input and output as in fig. 1 for basics 1 and 2.

[[nbasic 1 = basic 2, and v = basic 2 – basic 1, but basic 2 = u = nbasic 1, and v = nbasic 1 – basic 1]]

Fig. 3. An array of the elements of the Model of Universality related in attempt

v = (basic 1)(n - 1) = b1(n - 1), v = b(n - 1), but v + b $\leq$ u + s ---- **(1)**

A series of production or innovations without further enhancement is v + b = u + 0 = u, and v + b = u - --- (2), therefore, v = u – b [first basic (basic 1), is enhanced and remains constant without any more enhancement when s remains 0, thus s = 0]

1.19.1 IN A SERIES OF SLACK:

Input → Ξ → Output 1 → Ξ → Output 2 → Ξ Output n …

Fig. 4. As seen in figure fig. 1 above, Ξ represents a system and their evolving (evolutionary) resulting replicate(s) [i.e. valuable(s)], and → represents the inputs and the outputs of an activity/activities/basic(s) on the system.

Basic 1 → [Ξ Slack 1 Ξ] → Basic 2 → [Ξ Slack 2 Ξ] → Basic 3 → [Ξ Slack 3 Ξ] → Basic n → [Ξ Slack n Ξ] … Where, … implies "and so on".

Fig. 5. As seen in fig. 2 above, Ξ represents a system, $\rightarrow$ represents the input and the output basic(s)/activity/activities on the system(s), and the various resulting systems i.e. the evolutionary replica/replicates [valuable(s)], and [Ξ Slack 1 Ξ] represents the replicating "sense" of activities to or that instantiates (evokes) the evolution.

Figure 4 above represents the hypothetical abstract model of the more realistic model represented by that of figure 5. Therefore, $b1 < b2 < b3 < bn$ ..., and if $s = 0$ then, $b1 = b2 = b3 = bn$ ..., where, $b =$ basic, and $s =$ slack (the replicating activity that instantiates the evolution and therefore, the evolutionary replica/replicates).

Now, $b1 = b2 = b3 = bn$ ..., shows that, $b1 - b2 = b2 - b3 = b3 - bn$ ... $= 0$, this implies that (i.e. using the chain rule in mathematics), then $b1 - bn$, is also equaled to zero, that is, $b1 - bn = bn - b1 = 0$, and thus, mathematically, this also means that $b - bn = 0$, and hence $b = bn$.

Now again, when $s = 0$, then, $b - bn = bn - b = 0$, and $b - bn = b(1 - n)$, also, $bn - b = b(n - 1)$, which means that, $b - bn = b(1 - n) = bn - b = b(n - 1)$, therefore, $1 - n = n - 1$. This implies that, $1 + 1 = n + n$ implies that $2 = 2n$ and hence, [$n = 2/2 = 1$ hence $n = 1$] ---- **(6).**

This very result has a very important implication. From the whole deduction, we conclude that $n = 1$ is a result that indicates something is always the same, and since there are no constraints or constrains which is s thus in the interim put as ("$\pm s$" or "$+$ or $- s$"), it does not matter when b should equal bn, because, b, a basic, is still the same as several such basics $= u_i$ of the same element(s), or whether $b - bn$ should equal $bn - b$, for the same reason.

1.19.2 WHAT DO WE MEAN BY THAT? "If for the same basic elements without further enhancement in status or value (i.e. $s = 0$), equal amounts or things, or values, or basics, or activities are compared they are the same" ..... **[Deduction 1]**.

1.19.3 WHAT DOES DEDUCTION 1 MEAN? It means development remains at a constant or at a particular stagnant level where $s = 0$, $s =$ slack (i.e. activity/activities), which means development remains constant at that level, when development activities on a value in a system remains zero.

1.19.4 QUESTION OF VERIFICATION OF THEORY 1 (or DEDUCTION 1), FOR JUSTIFICATION: Is this result the same even if the activities are negative, or positive? We do not know yet, we must further verify to see if it works in a particular $+/-$ direction or both directions (i.e. justification). [Please look for the other volumes or versions of this paper to verify more empirical discoveries on value mechanics. This paper is the volume 1]. By version, we mean a more advanced project (the post-doctoral) write-ups.

1.19.5 VERIFICATION OF THEORY 1: Let us go back to $b - bn = 0 = bn - b$, if $s = 0$, in this case $s =$ slack (the activity/activities). We need to use one of the ends (LHS or RHS, where, LHS means left hand side, and RHS means right hand side) of the equation above, and since the LHS = RHS we can use anyone of them without affecting the result. We therefore, decide to use the RHS thus, $bn - b = 0$, in this case $bn - b = b (n - 1)$. Now, since $s = 0$, we put $b(n - 1) = 0 = b(n - 1)$, and $b(n - 1) = b(n - 1)$. This implies that, $b(n-1)/n(bn - b) = b(n-1)/ bn(n - 1) = b/bn$, and since $n = 1$, as firstly deduced, then $b/bn = b/b1 = b/b = 1$. Where, n is an integer representing the number of times or iterations. Value could be advanced, but through iterations n. This iterations could result into various degrees of value. However, value is inside advancement (development), meaning iterations could be repetitive processes leading to a high performance, achievement, or development, to enhance that value, provided the iterations are in the positive direction, if in the negative direction, then that direction should be favorable to advancement, otherwise there is an anomaly or insensitivity somewhere, there is no negativity in constraints of development up the advancement ladder.

1.19.6 WHAT DOES THIS MEAN? [b/bn], as indicated earlier on, implies that, "even if we take several of the same basic(s) together (bn) and of the same elements and compare this group to one out of them, s remaining zero, it is still the same basic and basic result and therefore, the same value in all (i.e. $b = bn = b1$)" ..... **[Deduction 2]**.

Therefore theory 1 above is justified by theory 2. That is, there is no much development up, but development remains at the same level or "worse (VERIFIABLE) depending on the rate of growth of size (e.g. population)" which depends on that same system or basic or limited resources, where development activities see no improvement than ever, and this phenomenon does not therefore, promote enhanced evolutionary replica/replicates. The opposite will happen when $s \neq 0$ and there will be development or growth of standards and benchmarks, e.g. comparing the current smart phones to all the previous and historic era phones and mobile devices.

1.20 FURTHER QUESTION OF VERIFICATION AND JUSTIFICATION IN THEORY

(DEDUCTION)

1.20.0 INTRODUCTION: If $s \neq 0$, then $u = b(n-1) \neq 0$, where, $u =$ a valuable and as we see the v as u indirectly in this case, v is proportional, or a factor, a multiple, a quotient, or an additive to u, depending on the field in use. However, if $s = 0$, then $b = bn$, where b is the basic at the time of evaluation. From the result in 'deduction 2', we see that, $b(n-1)/n(bn - b) = b(n-1)/ bn(n - 1) = b/bn$, and $b(n-1) = bn - b$, and when $s \neq 0$, then $bn(n - 1) \neq 0$ applies, so that, $v = bn(n - 1)$ implies that, $v = bn^2 - bn = n(bn - b)$, hence, $v = n(bn - b)$.

In this case, n = depends on time (n is a function of time), n is identical to frequency with respect to time. If n is identical to frequency timed, then v = depends on time too. Therefore, the value v is embedded in u the valuable. "Since n = 1, and b/bn = 1, value developed within a constant time period implies and/or depends on performance" .... **[Deduction 3]**

1.20.1 FURTHER EMPIRICAL DEDUCTION: $b = bn$ and $(b = bn)/bn ===> (b/bn) = (bn/bn) ===> b/bn = 1$, but from equation (6) above, $n = 1$. Hence, $(b/bn) = n$, such that, the first principle here considered n as an integer (i.e. $n = 1, 2, 3, 4 ...$), **where s = 0 in this case [means that, there is no advancement upon the first basic b]**

1.20.2 DEGREES OF FREEDOM: By degree of freedom here, we mean that, there is a chance or the means, or the capacity to improve. In this context, we classify three degrees of freedoms; 1) first degree of freedom, 2) second degree of freedom, and 3) third degree of freedom. The first degree of freedom is static no movement or progress in basic status, and the second and third degrees of freedom are respectively dynamic, they are movements, and progressions, in an exponential growth pattern. Then from the third degree of freedom, development continues unabated. Later unbelievable deductions in a post-doctoral review from this results showed that these expressions are possible.

Again where $s = 0$, in this case, and even though, $===> b/bn = 1$ ---- **(7)** is true, but it is also true where $s = 0$ that, $(bn/b) = 1$ ---- **(8)**, because as argued in [deduction 1], b and bn. are the same. This shows that, since $n = 1$, $(bn/b) = n$. Now, since the model is considered a flexible one, $(bn/b) = 1/n$ ---- **(9)** is also true. Also, $u = nbasic\ 1 = bn = basic\ 2$ ---- **(10)**, and $v = basic\ 2 - basic\ 1$, but since basic $2 = nbasic\ 1$, then, $v = nbasic\ 1 - basic\ 1$, where basic $1 = basic = b$. By section 1.12.3, we could imagine $s \to n$ - --- **(11)**.

1.20.3 FIRST DEGREE OF FREEDOM: We continue to multiply $[(bn/b) = 1/n]$ by n, we have $[(bn/b) = 1/n]\ (n^q)$, where q = increasing exponent (i.e. $q = 1, 2, 3, 4 ...$). Now, when $q = 1$ then, $[(bn/b) = 1/n]n^q = [(bn/b) = 1/n]\ n^1 = (bn^2/b) = 1$. ------- **[Deduction 3]**.

The first principle on basics ends on [Deduction 3], because no matter what, the result is always $n = 1$ from here. **Prove:** $[(bn^2/b) = 1](n^q)$ always boils down to the same $(bn^2/b) = 1$ [this is an interesting phenomenon], no matter the effect of (n^q) on the result, hence, we need to move on to another degree of freedom which is the second degree of freedom, if we want to start realizing some meaningful results on value enhancement. $[(bn^2/b) = 1]n = [(bn^3/b) = n]$, $[(bn^3/b) = n]n = [(bn^4/b) = n^2]$,

$[(bn^4/b) = n^2]n = [(bn^5/b) = n^3]...$ Now, you will realize that, $[(bn^2/b) = 1] = [(bn^3/b) = n] = [(bn^4/b) = n^2] = [(bn^5/b) = n^3]$ ... (therefore, no change! The resulting algebra is still leaving n^2 inclusive in each square bracket.

Again, this is, [First degree of freedom (there is still no change in circumstances, no development, no constraints, stagnation, no restrictions, and no innovations) and in this case n^q does not have any effect on the results, even when q = 1, 2, 3 … ∞ (this also means that, n^q, is such that $n^q = n^{1, 2, 3 … ∞}$), and this will never affect the result of (bn/b = 1/n)(n^q)], such as [(bn²/b) = 1, where q = 1, or where q = 1, 2, 3, …], simply, the result will remain constant.

1.20.4 SECOND DEGREE OF FREEDOM: There should be a restriction. This means that some development has begun. There is thinking, there is discovery, there is innovation, there is improvement, simply, and there is an enhancement of value from the first degree of freedom to the second degree of freedom in order to improve. In this case, b is no more equal to bn. we now have b and b2, and b < b2 ===> b2 is higher in value status than b, and b2 is a valuable the second basic, and b is also a valuable the first basic, but b2 is an improved b, (e.g. b is like a sheet of blank white paper, but if a photo is printed on the white paper, then, it is no more b, but it is now b2). In this case, when q = 1 then, [(bn/b) = 1/n](n^q) = [(bn/b) = 1/n](n^1) = [(bn²/b) = 1], changes to become [(nb2/b) = 1/n](n^q) = [(nb2/b) = 1/n]n^1 = [(n²b2/b) = 1]. … **[Deduction 4].**

From [deduction 4] we can conclude that, [(n²b2/b) = 1] algebraically boils down to [(n² /b)(b2) = 1] = [(b 2) = (b/n²)], this is a very important result which shows that the second degree of freedom of value enhancement can continue from that level unabated, once the frequency or the number of cycles (n) progresses, and the version (b2) will continue to grow sequentially at that second degree level. This is because at the first principle level of basics, we have b whose n = 1and b remains constant and even b = bn., **but at the second degree level, limits are set, and these limits no more allow n to continue to be 1 in value, but less**. We presume that, since we are dealing with a model which is universal or flexible, n might also, be more than 1 (i.e. n > 1), depending on the situation. **However, for now, we are working with n < 1**. Therefore, the constrained n is identical to frequency is identical to 3.2×10^{-8} cycles/sec for every 1 version of value enhanced. We would see how this value was obtained later.

The second degree of freedom is dynamic, in this case n^q does have effect on the results, even when q = 1, 2, 3 … ∞ (this also means that, n^q, is such that $n^q = n^{1, 2, 3 … ∞}$), and this will affect the result of [(bn/b) = 1/n] (n^q). Simply, the result will remain dynamic and progressive. For instance, [(nb2/b) = 1/n] n^q = [(nb2/b) = 1/n] (n^1) = [(n²b2 / b) = 1], and when $n^q = n^{1, 2, 3 … ∞}$, where, q = 1, 2, 3 … ∞, then, the result will grow as follows; [($n^{1, 2, 3 … ∞}$) (b1, 2, 3 … ∞)]/b = 1/($n^{1, 2, 3 … ∞}$)]($n^{1, 2, 3 … ∞}$) = [[($n^{1, 2, 3 … ∞}$) (b1, 2, 3 … ∞)] ($n^{(1, 2, 3 … ∞)}$) / b = $n^{(1, 2, 3 … ∞) - 1}$]………………**[Deduction 5]**.

This expressions in deduction 5 were left to remain as it is to prove that, at least changes in n could have an effect on the result at b2 the "second degree of freedom". At least, we can see that, when n^q is growing exponentially $1/n^q$ is growing and q = 1, 2, 3…∞, when n = 3.2×10^{-8}. For instance, 1/n = 1/ (3.2×10^{-8}) = 31,250,000 and when n grows to n², we have $1/n^2$ = 1/ $(3.2 \times 10^{-8})^2$ = 9.765625×10^{14} =

34

976,562,500,000,000, that is [976.6 trillion!], imagine the superfluous figure change! Similarly, the figure will grow progressively if we allow n to increase as 2n, 3n, 4n…∞n. We will see this elaboration below under 3rd degree of freedom.

Similarly as we see above, $[(n^2b2/b) = 1]$ boils down to $[(n^2/b)(b2) = 1] = [(b2) = (b/n^2)]$, from [deduction 5] we can conclude that, $[(n^{1,2,3…∞})$ $(b1, 2, 3 … ∞)]/b = 1/(n^{1,2,3…∞})](n^{1,2,3…∞}) = [[(n^{1,2,3…∞})(b1, 2, 3 … ∞)](n^{(1,2,3…∞)})/b = n^{(1,2,3…∞)-1}]$ is finally, $[(b1, 2, 3 … ∞) = b/n^{(1,2,3…∞)}]$, and this shows that, $n^{(1,2,3…∞)}$ grows exponentially and causes the versions [b1, 2, 3 … ∞] to also, progressively grow. [Deduction 5], will now lead us to the 3rd degree of freedom.

1.20.5 THIRD DEGREE OF FREEDOM: As stated earlier on, the 3rd degree of freedom is also dynamic and progressive however, b2 < b3==> b3 is higher in value status than b2, and b3 is a valuable, the third basic, and b2 is also a valuable the second basic, but b3 is an improved b2, [e.g. b2 is like a sheet of blank white paper with a photo printed on the white paper, then, b3 is like several similar other photo cards stacked on this one sheet of paper, but serves as an album that is capable of viewing by slides, (can you imagine this incredibility?), meaning that b3 is an improved version of b2. E.g. Microsoft documents 2013 (similar to the explanation on b3) is an improved version of MS document 2010 (such as explained of b2)]. In this case, when q = 1 then, $(bn/b = 1/n)n^q = (bn/b = 1/n)n^1 = (bn^2/b) = 1$, in the case of b → b = b1, and changes in the 2nd degree of freedom to become $(nb2 / b = 1/n)n^q = (nb2/b = 1/n)n^1 = (n^2b2/b) = 1$ in the case of b → b2 and continue to grow at that level e.g. (b2)I, (b2)II, (b2)III, (b2)IV…(b2)∞, which also changes in the 3rd degree of freedom to become $(n^3b3/b) = 1$, in the case of b2 → b3 …… [Deduction 6].

Similarly as we see above in the second degree of freedom, the third degree of freedom in [deduction 6] shows finally that, $[(n^2b3/b) = 1]$ algebraically boils down to $[(n^2/b)(b3) = 1] = [(b3) = (b/n^2)]$. This is a very important result which shows that the third degree of freedom of value enhancement can continue from that level unabated for example [(b3)I, (b3)II, (b3)III, (b3)IV…(b3)∞], once the frequency or the number of cycles (n) progresses, and the version (b3) will continue to grow sequentially at that third degree level [(b3)I, (b3)II, (b3)III, (b3)IV…(b3)∞].

Now, from [deduction 5] we can conclude that, $[(n^{1,2,3…∞})(b1, 2, 3 … ∞)]/b = 1/(n^{1,2,3…∞})](n^{1,2,3…∞}) = [[(n^{1,2,3…∞})(b1, b2, b3 … b∞)](n^{(1,2,3…∞)})/b = n^{(1,2,3…∞)-1}]$ is finally, $[(b1, b2, b3 … b∞) = b/n^{(1,2,3…∞)}]$, and this shows that, $n^{(1,2,3…∞)}$ grows exponentially and causes the versions [b1, b2, b3 … b∞] to also, grow progressively.

1.20.6 NOTE: Each level of the respective b1, b2, b3 … b∞ is growing as from b2 onwards as of (b2)I, (b2)II, (b2)III, (b2)IV…(b2)∞, and (b3)I, (b3)II, (b3)III, (b3)IV…(b3)∞ and (b4)I, (b4)II, (b4)III, (b4)IV… (b4)∞, and so on. As stated before, the case of b1 will grow, but it is still the same basic and the result remains constant, no other advanced versions of the system which is growing or advancing apply.

Again, it is after this third degree of freedom similarly as is the case with the second degree of freedom, that we have, $[(n^{1, 2, 3 \, \cdots \, \infty})$ (b1, 2, 3 … $\infty)] / b = 1/ (n^{1, 2, 3 \, \cdots \, \infty})$ …∞ as shown above in [deduction 5], and development continues unabated from this stage, meaning that, value increases unabated, simply, value is enhanced continuously and progressively and exponentially. However, if we take a look at the exponential n growth, we would realize that the growth of n is always quadratic at n^2, but n itself changes in this case upwards or downwards, e.g. n becomes 1n, 2n, 3n … ∞n. Therefore, $[(n^{1, 2, 3 \, \cdots \, \infty})$ (b1, 2, 3 … $\infty)] / b = 1/ (n^{1, 2, 3 \, \cdots \, \infty})$ …∞, was as such expressed to shows that there is continuous growth, but the growth in n is discontinued at n^2.

1.20.7 PROVE: With, for instance b2, ($n^2b2/b = 1$), and continuous-growth from here is ($n^2b2/b = 1)n^q$, meaning q = 1 gives ($n^3b2/b = n$). Then, ($n^3b2/b = n$) will further grow as ($n^3b2/b = n)n$, when q = 2, giving ($n^4b2/b = n^2$). Then, ($n^4b2/b = n^2$) will grow further as ($n^4b2/b = n^2$) n, when q = 3, to become ($n^5b2/b = n^3$) and so on in a similar manner. The result of all these produce mathematically and by algebra the same n^2 in each of the sequential terms. Just take a moment and compute by indices to see this reality.

For instance, in the case of Moore's law, this result proves that Moore's law is true. According to Wikipedia.org, (update 2014), **"Moore's law"** is the observation that, over the history of **computing hardware**, the number of **transistors** in a dense **integrated circuit**, doubles approximately every two years. The observation is named after **Gordon E. Moore**, co-founder of the **Intel Corporation**, who first described the trend in a 1965 paper and formulated its current statement in 1975".

For exponential growth aspect, and at the Intel.com, it was also stated there that, "The future of Moore's Law could deliver a magnitude of exponential capability increases, driving a fundamental shift in computing, networking, storage, and communication devices to handle the ever-growing digital content and Intel's vision of 15 billion intelligent, connected devices". The model of universality "v + b ≤ u + s", having been considered a flexible model, hence in [deduction 5] under section 1.20.6, we see exponential growth as a possibility, and we will see this as a graph in subsequent volumes in the methodology section of this paper.

1.20.8 SUMMARY ON THE DEGREES OF FREEDOM AS A WHOLE: Preambles; According to the muv equation (1) above, $v + b \le u + s$, rewriting this in the form of $y \le f(x)$, we have $v \le f(u, b, s)$, or $v = f(u, b, s)$ where $s = 0$ according to section 1.14 above, where b is negative. Where, $v = f(u, b, s)$ generally represents a system, its values and function. However, $v = f(u, b, s) \rightarrow v = u + (-b) + s$. Since this represents the muv, $v + b \le u + s$ represent a general equation w.r.t. the muv and everything "n" and of values ranging from 0 to ∞ where, v = value, b = basic, u = valuable, and s = slack. However, as by [deduction 3] i.e. section 1.20.0, $n = 1$ therefore, $n = 0 \ldots \infty \rightarrow n = 1 \ldots \infty$ since n ranges from 1 to ∞, hence, $v = f(u, b, s) \rightarrow v = u + (-b) + s$ such that, $\sum_{n=1}^{n=\infty} v \rightarrow f(\sum_{n=1}^{n=\infty} u, \sum_{n=1}^{n=\infty} b, \sum_{n=1}^{n=\infty} s) = \sum_{n=1}^{n=\infty} u + \sum_{n=1}^{n=\infty} (-b) + \sum_{n=1}^{n=\infty} s)$, in the lim: $n \rightarrow \infty$ then, $\sum_{n=1}^{n=\infty} v = \sum_{n=1}^{n=\infty} u + \sum_{n=1}^{n=\infty} (-b) + \sum_{n=1}^{n=\infty} s = \sum_{n=1}^{n=\infty} (u + (-b) + s) \rightarrow \int_{n=1}^{n=\infty} v dv \rightarrow \int_{n=1}^{n=\infty} u du + \int_{n=1}^{n=\infty} (-b) db + \int_{n=1}^{n=\infty} s ds$. **Now;** by equation (10), section 1.20.2, $u = bn$, and by equation (11) $s \rightarrow n$. The changing effect on a basic b, and on a valuable u, is multiplication effect or (product effect), and this product effect is rather additive in accounting such as explained in section 1.6, and the extraction of value v out of a valuable effect is an additive effect i.e. $v \le bn + (-b) = bn - b$, further, $v \le f(u, b, s)$, but lim: $v \rightarrow \infty$, $s \rightarrow \infty$, $u \rightarrow \infty$, then, $v = f(u, b, s) \rightarrow v = u + (-b) + s \rightarrow v = u + (-b) = (bn - b)$ where $s = 0$, and further-v is given by $v \rightarrow vn = u - b + s_1 \Rightarrow vn = v_1 = (bn-b)n = b(n^2-n)$ this is a multiplicative effect from s_1 "= or =>" n, where $s_1 > 0$. Also, further-u $\rightarrow$ un = either u_1, u_2, or $u_3 \ldots$ is such that un = $b + v_1 = b(bn-b)n = b.b(n^2-n) = b^2(n^2 - n) = u_2$ --- where a multiplicative effect here, is taking place in the product. This chain is similar in u_2, u_3 --- therefore, u = bn => $u_1 = b^2(n^2 - n)$ ---- **(12),** that is, u ascending as u^1, u^2, u^3 respectively --- whereas v rises too, due to further-s ascensions.

Now, we have $\int_{n=1}^{n=\infty} f(n) dn \rightarrow \int_{n=1}^{n=\infty} (bn - b)n \, dn = b \int_{n=1}^{n=\infty} (n.n - n) \, dn = b \left[\left(\frac{n^3}{3} \right) - \frac{n^2}{2} \right] + c$ (we ignored the limits 1 to ∞ because we wanted to obtain a general view of the formula, whereas, applying the limits would have eliminated the formula away from the shape we wanted to see it, hence, $b \left[\left(\frac{n^3}{3} \right) - \frac{n^2}{2} \right] + c$). If we hold b constant at b = 1 then we have the whole formula turning into $\left[\left(\frac{n^3}{3} \right) - \frac{n^2}{2} \right] + c$. This is just the third degree equation of value, modified as such, which we will see in volume two of this book. From the third degree equation of value, we can arrive at the first degree equation by the use of the second degree equation of value. Further explanation would be done on this section on "degrees of freedom" in the subsequent volumes by way of throwing more light into its understanding. This is a real powerful formula where we still have a meaning for value even if we put $v = 1$ and $b = 1$, usually, growth actually begins when we put $n = 2$ with the above formula, and that depicts Moore's law where, in an exponential growth given by $y = e_i^x$ where the number of **transistors** in a dense **integrated circuit**, doubles approximately every two years.

RECOMMENDATION AND CONCLUSION

5.0 INTRODUCTION: The model $b + v \leq u + s$ as expressed in sections 1.1 and 3.0 is a fluid that could be used to express every system, we believe. Every system could be broken down into four solid blocks b, v, u, and s, where b = basic, v = value, u = valuable, and s = slack. Seeing the characteristics curves explained above in chapter 4 (this chapter could be seen in the original dissertation if we could trace the original of 170 pages or read subsequent volumes II, III, & IV of almost 45 pages each), we could recommend that VTPU: V = virtual, T = theory, P = practice/ materialism, and U = the unseen in section 3.0 is about everything the universe could hold. The meeting point of all these necessitates a deep school into **value mechanics** programs to help relate every expressions to one another, so that the deep understanding of one thing could be possible through another, E.g. so that, we could understand V through U, through T, and through P and so much of fluid among them systematically, streamlining-wise, logically, methodically, analytically, and synthesis/ synthetic.

5.1 With $v = 1/(1 - n) = 1/(1 - b/u)$ first degree value, $v = - n^2$ second degree value, $n^3 - n^2 - 1 = 0$ third degree value, Amdahl's Law, section 3.2.1, Gustafson's Law, section 3.2.3, we recommend that, the order of importance of various systems or resources in a system could be compared such as of the expression in section 3.4.4 second and third paragraphs. This could see application in political ratings, ratings of extend of the development of countries or people, computer systems, or software, also, in engineering, economics and more. Also, the valuables of a system to be developed could be predicted using n, where n is a factor of value, a valuable, or a strategy "s" termed in this paper as slack. Thus if b is 1, and u is unknown, but n is considered as 10 years/ 1 year, then $n = u/b ===> u = (b)(n) = 1 \times 10$ = 10 valuable-units [i.e. predicted]. We did not want to distort information therefore, we allowed the notations of the sections to remain as it were, because we had as much as almost 170 pages in the original dissertation, and to get a requirement of 45 pages for publication prerequisite, then we needed to do cut and pastes. The sections and sub-sections notations were as of the original and if we could trace the original dissertation of 170 pages then we could go straight to the sections stated or noted here in this paper or book. This work was a discovery leading to theoretical physics that proved our universe and realized that what Einstein, Schrodinger, Hubble, Hawkins, etc. said were all nothing but the truth. This work was just but one of the volumes (the 1st volume) of 4 volumes that will be obtained when we complete breaking down the original volume of 170 pages into 45 pages each in order to fulfill the publication requirement. This work is the beginning of a new theory "Value Mechanics" and the title above of this very paper stated, "Forerunning Value Mechanics", therefore, this work is a forerunner of the value mechanics itself that is coming in a title dabbed as "Value Mechanics: An Introduction", and further work following this later title is the grand "value mechanics" that will be entitled "Value Mechanics". The post-doctoral work on this is already underway.

BIBLIOGRAPHY
6.0 BIBLIOGRAPHY

1. a) HUSQVARNA GROUP (2013), Date revisited the site (11th May, 2013), Website: http://husqvarnagroup.com/en/ir/financial-data/key-ratio-definitions and, b) Cash Focus (2013), Date revisited the site (11th May, 2013), Website: http://www.cashfocus.com/financial-analysis.htm and, c) ,http://www.docstoc.com/docs/70831231/Executing-E-Business-Strategies-the-Ge-Way

2. Allaboutcircuits.com or Halloelectronics.com (2012), Date visited the website (7th May, 2013), Website: http://www.allaboutcircuits.com/vol_2/chpt_1/6.html

3. Allaboutcircuits.com or Halloelectronics.com (2012), Date visited the site (7th May, 2013), Website: http://www.allaboutcircuits.com/vol_2/chpt_1/6.html

4. Amos Web Encyclopedia (2013), Date visited site (11th May, 2013), Website: http://www.amosweb.com/cgi-bin/awb_nav.pl?s=wpd&c=dsp&k=economic+profit

5. Angelfire, Date visited the website (3rd May, 2013), Website: http://www.angelfire.com/oh5/wordstems/word_stems2.html

6. ASQ, (). What is Quality Function Deployment? Date visited the website (July 6, 2016). Retrieved from: http://asq.org/learn-about-quality/qfd-quality-function-deployment/overview/overview.html

7. Boundless.com, []. Solid to Gas Phase Transition. Date visited the website [June 19, 2016]. Website: https://www.boundless.com/chemistry/textbooks/boundless-chemistry-textbook/liquids-and-solids-11/phase-changes-90/solid-to-gas-phase-transition-393-6578/

8. Businessdictionary.com (2013), Date visited the website (27th April, 2013), Website: www.businessdictionary.com/definition/value.html

9. Chemical Heritage Foundation, (2010 - 2016). Amedeo Avogadro. Date visited the website (July 3, 2016). Retrieved from: http://www.chemheritage.org/discover/online-resources/chemistry-in-history/themes/the-path-to-the-periodic-table/avogadro.aspx

10. Chemistry Texas A & M University: ATM, (2015). Periodic Table of Elements. Date visited the website (March 23, 2015). Retrieved from: https://www.chem.tamu.edu/academics/fyp/educator_resources/isotopes_introduction.php

11. DEFITIONS.NET (2013), Date visited the site (28th April, 2013), Website: www.definitions.net/definition/valuable

12. Dictionary.cambridge.org (2013), Date visited the website (27th April, 2013), Website: www.dictionary.cambridge.org/dictionary/british/basics?q=basics

13. Dictionary.cambridge.org (2013), Date visited the website (27th April, 2013), Website: www.dictionary.cambridge.org/dictionary/british/valuable_1?q=valuable

14. Dictionary.reference.com (2013), Date visited the website (27th April, 2013), Website: http://dictionary.reference.com/browse/commodity

15. Dictionary.reference.com (2013), Date visited the website (27th April, 2013), Website: www.dictionary.reference.com/browse/basics

16. Free Dictionary by FARLEX, (2003-2014). Forte. Date visited the website (December 27, 2014). Retrieved from: http://www.thefreedictionary.com/forte

17. G. Dennis Beecroft, Grace L. Duffy, and John W. Moran, (2003). The Executive Guide to Improvement and Change. USA. ASQ Quality Press. Date visited the website (January 2, 2015). Retrieved from: www.asq.org/learn-about-quality/problem-solving/overview.html

18. Galileo Physics, Date visited the site (7th of May, 2013), Website: http://galileo.phys.virginia.edu/classes/241L/emwaves/emwaves.htm and WHO (2013), Date visited the site (7th of May, 2013) http://www.who.int/peh-emf/about/WhatisEMF/en/

19. Galileo Physics, Date visited the website (7th of May, 2013), Website: http://galileo.phys.virginia.edu/classes/241L/emwaves/emwaves.htm

20. George Boeree (2003), Date visited the website (3rd of May, 2013), Organization: Webspace.ship.edu, Website: http://webspace.ship.edu/cgboer/morphology.html

21. George Boeree (2003), Date visited the website (3rd of May, 2013), Organization: Webspace.ship.edu, Website: http://webspace.ship.edu/cgboer/morphology.html

22. Higgins et al (2012), The Impact of Digital Technology on Learning: A Summary for the Education Foundation Endowment, Date visited the site (8th May, 2013), Website: http://educationendowmentfoundation.org.uk/uploads/pdf/The_Impact_of_Digital_Technolog ies_on_Learning_(2012).pdf

23. Higgins et al (2012), The Impact of Digital Technology on Learning: A Summary for the Education Foundation Endowment, Date visited the site (8th May, 2013), Website: http://educationendowmentfoundation.org.uk/uploads/pdf/The_Impact_of_Digital_Technologies_on _Learning_(2012).pdf

24. Howstuffworks.com (2013), Date visited site (06/05/2013), Website: http://www.howstuffworks.com/atom8.htm

25. Howstuffworks.com (2013), Date visited site (06/05/2013), Website: http://www.howstuffworks.com/atom8.htm

26. IEC, (2016). International Electro-technical Commission. Date visited the website (July 6, 2016). Retrieved from: www.sensorcentral.com/worldsupport/standards01.php or http://www.keyence.com/ss/products/sensor/sensorbasics/

27. IEEE, (2016).Institute of Electrical and Electronic Engineers. Date visited the website (July 6, 2016). Retrieved from: www.ieee.org

28. Illinois SPDG (State Personnel Development Grant). Problem Solving Method of Decision Making. Date visited the website (February 8, 2015). Retrieved from: http://www.illinoisrti.org/i-rti-network/for-educators/understanding-rti-mtss/problem-solving-process

29. Informationbuilder.com (2013), Date visited the website (26th April, 2013), Website: www.informationbuilder.com/kpi-key-performance-indicators

30. Intel.com, (). Moore's Law and Intel Innovation. Date visited the website (February 28, 2015). Retrieved from: http://www.intel.com/content/www/us/en/history/museum-gordon-moore-law.html

31. INVESTOPEDIA (2013), Date visited the site (11th May, 2013), Website: http://www.investopedia.com/terms/e/economicprofit.asp

32. Investopedia.com (2013), Date visited the website (27th April, 2013), Website: www.investopedia.com/terms/c/commodity.asp

33. Investorwords.com (2013), Date visited the website (27th April, 2013), Website: www.investorwords.com/s209/value.html

34. Investorwords.com (2013), Date visited the website (27th April, 2013), Website: www.investorwords.com/975/commodity.html

35. Jessica Keyes, (2003). Software Engineering Handbook. USA. CRC Press LLC.

36. K. A. Stroud, (2007). Engineering Mathematics. Seventh Edition. Macmillan Education Ltd. London.

37. Laine et al (), what is Computer Programing? Date visited the site (8th May, 2013), Website: http://www.bfoit.org/itp/Programming.html

38. Laine et al (), What is Computer Programing? Date visited the site (8th May, 2013), Website: http://www.bfoit.org/itp/Programming.html

39. Language Characteristics- University of Minnesota Duluth (2010), Date visited the website (3rd May, 2013), Website: http://ppt.linux5.net/l/language-characteristics---university-of-minnesota-duluth-welcomes-you-w223-ppt.ppt

40. Language Characteristics- University of Minnesota Duluth (2010), Date visited the website (3rd May, 2013), Website: http://ppt.linux5.net/l/language-characteristics---university-of-minnesota-duluth-welcomes-you-w223-ppt.ppt

41. Margaret H. Hamilton and William A. Packer, (2007). Universal Language System for Preventative Systems Engineering. Cambridge. Hamilton Technologies Inc. Date visited the website (December 14, 2014). Website: http://www.htius.com/Articles/36.pdf

42. Mariam Webster (2013), Date visited the site (3rd May, 2013), Website: http://www.merriam-webster.com/dictionary/phonology

43. Mariam Webster (2013), Date visited the site (3rd May, 2013), Website: http://www.merriam-webster.com/dictionary/phonology

44. Mathsfun.com (2011), Date visited the site (11th May, 2013), Website: www.mathsfun.com/measure/index.html

45. Merriam-Webster Incorporated Dictionary, (2015). Probability. Date visited the website (March 23, 2015). Retrieved from: http://www.merriam-webster.com/dictionary/probability

46. Mihir A. et al (2006), EVA- Economic Value Added, Date revisited website (10th May, 2013), Website: http://www.studymode.com/essays/Eva-Economic-Value-Added-1280572.html

47. Mises.org (2013), Date visited the website (27th April, 2013), Website: http://mises.org/Community/blogs/lilburne/archive/2009/06/19/224245.aspx

48. Moses Bean et al: Leaderru.com (2008), The Image of the Creator, Date visited the website (8th May, 2013), Website: http://www.leaderu.com/theology/image_creator.html

49. Moses Bean et al: Leaderru.com (2008), The Image of the Creator, Date visited the site (8th May, 2013), Website: http://www.leaderu.com/theology/image_creator.html

50. Name of the website: Angelfire, Date visited (3rd May, 2013), Website: http://www.angelfire.com/oh5/wordstems/word_stems2.html

51. Nicholas Nigroponte (1995), Date visited the site (06/05/2013), Website: http://en.wikipedia.org/wiki/Digital_economy

52. Nicholas Nigroponte (1995), Date visited the site (06/05/2013), Website: http://en.wikipedia.org/wiki/Digital_economy

53. Online Cambridge Dictionary (2011), Date revisited the site (11th May, 2013), Website: http://dictionary.cambridge.org/dictionary/british/measurement?q=measurement

54. Oxford Dictionary.com (2011), Date revisited the site (11th May, 2013), Website: www.oxforddictionaries.com/definition/measurement

55. Oxforddictionary.com (2013), Date visited the website 27th April, 2013(), Website: www.oxforddictionaries.com/definitions/basic

56. Oxforddictionary.com (2013), Date visited the website 27th April, 2013(), Website: www.oxforddictionaries.com/definition/valuable

57. Pamela Peterson Drake of James Madison University (1997), Date revisited site (10th May, 2013), Website: www.educ.jmu.edu/---drakepp/value/notes.htm

58. PEW Internet and American Life Project (2013), Date visited the site (8th May, 2013), Website: http://pewinternet.org/Reports/2013/Arts-and-technology/Main-Report/Section-6.aspx

59. PEW Internet and American Life Project (2013), Date visited the site (8th May, 2013), Website: http://pewinternet.org/Reports/2013/Arts-and-technology/Main-Report/Section-6.aspx

60. Physicsclass.com (2013), Date visited the site (7th May, 2013), Website: http://www.physicsclassroom.com/Class/sound/u1l11c.cfm

61. PRWEB Online Visibility From Focus (2013), Date visited the site (8th May, 2013), Website: http://www.prweb.com/releases/2013/2/prweb10480882.htm

62. PRWEB Online Visibility From Focus (2013), Date visited the site (8th May, 2013), Website: http://www.prweb.com/releases/2013/2/prweb10480882.htm

63. Quora.com, (Feb 8, 2016). What is the difference between the triple point and the critical point? Date visited the website [June 19, 2016]. Website: https://www.quora.com/What-is-difference-between-triple-point-and-critical-point

64. Reh (2013), Management.about.com, Date visited the website (26th April, 2013), Website: http://management.about.com/cs/generalmanagement/a/keyperfindic.htm

65. Richard P. Feynman (1985): Friesian.com (2013), Date visited the site (8th May, 2013), Website: http://www.friesian.com/quanta.htm

66. Richard P. Feynman (1985): Friesian.com (2013), Date visited the site (8th May, 2013), Website: http://www.friesian.com/quanta.htm

67. Sciencebuddies.org (2012), Date visited the site (10th May, 2013), Website: http://www.sciencebuddies.org/science-fair-projects/project_scientific_method.shtml

68. Sciencebuddies.org, (2002-2015). Steps of the Scientific Method. Date visited the website (February 1, 2015). Retrieved from: http://www.sciencebuddies.org/science-fair-projects/project_scientific_method.shtml

69. Stephen G. Powell, and Robert J. Batt, (2008). Modelling for Insight a Master Class for Business Analysts. Hoboken, New Jersey and Canada. John Wiley & Sons, Inc.

70. The New York Times (2012), Technology Affecting How Students Learn- Teachers Say, Date visited the site (8th May, 2013), Website: http://www.nytimes.com/2012/11/01/education/technology-is-changing-how-students-learn-teachers-say.html?pagewanted=all&_r=0

71. The New York Times (2012), Technology Affecting How Students Learn- Teachers Say, Date visited the site (8th May, 2013), Website: http://www.nytimes.com/2012/11/01/education/technology-is-changing-how-students-learn-teachers-say.html?pagewanted=all&_r=0

72. Thephysicsclassroom.com, Date visited the site (06/05/2013), Website: http://www.physicsclassroom.com/Class/sound/u11l2a.cfm

73. Thephysicsclassroom.com, Date visited the site (06/05/2013), Website: http://www.physicsclassroom.com/Class/sound/u11l2a.cfm and http://www.physicsclassroom.com/Class/sound/u11l1c.cfm

74. Thesaurus.yourdictionary.com (2013), Date visited the website (27th April, 2013), Website: http://thesaurus.yourdictionary.com/basics

75. TutorVista.com (2010), Date visited the site (7th of May, 2013), Website: http://physics.tutorvista.com/electricity-and-magnetism/electromagnet.html

76. TutorVista.com (2010), Date visited the site (7th of May, 2013), Website: http://physics.tutorvista.com/electricity-and-magnetism/electromagnet.html

77. UKESSAYS.COM (2003-2013),The UK's Expert Provider of Custom Essays, Date visited the site (13th May, 2013), Website: http://www.ukessays.com/essays/business/an-explanation-of-key-performance-indicators-business-essay.php and, Scott (2013), Calibre-elite.com, Date visited the website (26th April, 2013), Website: www.calibre-elite.com/keyperformance-areas.php

78. University of South Australia, (August 17, 2012). Data Collection and Analysis. Date visited the website (July 6, 2016). Retrieved from: http://w3.unisa.edu.au/researchstudents/milestones/data.asp

79. Vangie Beal, (2014). System. Date visited the website (December 2, 2015). Retrieved from: www.webopedia.com/TERM/S/system.html (copyright 2014)

80. W. R. Bennette, Date visited the site (8th May, 2013), Website: http://www3.alcatel-lucent.com/bstj/vol27-1948/articles/bstj27-3-446.pdf

81. W. R. Bennette, Date visited the site (8th May, 2013), Website: http://www3.alcatel-lucent.com/bstj/vol27-1948/articles/bstj27-3-446.pdf

82. Wayne L. Winston and S. Cristian Albright, (2007). Practical Management Science. Third Edition. USA. Thomson South-Western.

83. WHO (2013), Date visited the site (7th of May, 2013) http://www.who.int/peh-emf/about/WhatisEMF/en/

84. Wikipedia (2013), Date visited the site (3rd of May, 2013), Wesite: http://en.wikipedia.org/wiki/Infix

85. Wikipedia (2013), Date visited the site (3rd of May, 2013), Wesite: http://en.wikipedia.org/wiki/Infix

86. Wikipedia (2013), Date visited the site (4th of May, 2013), Website: http://en.wikipedia.org/wiki/Root_word

87. Wikipedia (2013), Date visited the site (4th of May, 2013), Website: http://en.wikipedia.org/wiki/Root_word

88. Wikipedia, (Update 2014). Systems Engineering. Date visited the website (December 22, 2014). Retrieved from: http://en.wikipedia.org/wiki/Systems_engineering

89. Wikipedia.org (2016). IDEFO. Date visited the website (July 6, 2016). Retrieved from: https://en.wikipedia.org/wiki/IDEF0

90. Wikipedia.org, (2016). IEEE 1284. Date visited the website (July 6, 2016). Retrieved from: https://en.wikipedia.org/wiki/IEEE_1284

91. Wikipedia.org, (Updated 2014). Moore's Law. Date visited the website (February 28, 2015). Retrieved from: http://en.wikipedia.org/wiki/Moore%27s_law

92. Wiktionary.org, Date visited website (3rd May, 2013), Website: http://en.wiktionary.org/wiki/syntax

93. Wiktionary.org, Date visited website (3rd May, 2013), Website: http://en.wiktionary.org/wiki/syntax

94. Willian M. K. Trochin (2006), Research Methods Knowledge Based (Measurement), Date revisited the site (11th May, 2013), Website: www.socialresearchmethods.net/kb/measurephp

95. Wolfgang (2000), Date visited the site (8th May, 2013), Website: http://www2.uni-jena.de/welsch/Papers/VirtualTBW.html

96. Wolfgang (2000), Date visited the site (8th May, 2013), Website: http://www2.uni-jena.de/welsch/Papers/VirtualTBW.html

YOUR KNOWLEDGE HAS VALUE

- We will publish your bachelor's and
  master's thesis, essays and papers

- Your own eBook and book -
  sold worldwide in all relevant shops

- Earn money with each sale

Upload your text at www.GRIN.com
and publish for free